Soul And The World

Vasanthi Isaacs

BookLeaf
Publishing
India | USA | UK

Made with ❤ on the BookLeaf Publishing Platform

www.bookleafpub.in

www.bookleafpub.com

Dedication

Dedicated to

My family:
My husband, daughter,
and grand daughter.

Preface

A collection of **poems** to tuck away in your hand.
To **awaken** you to **soul stirring** moments all around.
Some light and **lifting,** to leave you **smiling**
Some dark or deep to send you **thinking.**
But all in all an **offering** to **revive**, restore and **delight.**

Acknowledgements

Write angle

21 day challenge

Oct 2024

1. Turning water into wine

Turning water into wine,
Finding Joy amid the grind,
Dancing rainbows in muddy puddles,
Lilting tune snips in subway muddles,
Sweet perfumes past city fumes,
Tasting ice cream in winding queues,
Smiling, dimpled through tantrum tears,
Staying brave amid the fears,
Sensing a million stories around,
Tripping, sharing a steadying hand,
Whispering, thankful for strangers'- kind,
Ending day with grace abounding,
Finding Joy amid the grind,
Turning water into wine.

2. Pink to soul

Pink rain lilies,
On a grey drizzly morn,
Pink clean lotus,
In the stagnant pond,
Pink bougainvillea,
On a tall spiked wall,
Pink roses all shades,
Amid a garden of guards.

Pink cotton candy,
Pink bubblegum,
Pink tinted coolers,
Pink champagne in tall glasses.

Pink dress or a hat,
Or a raincoat too,
Pink shoes or socks,
A bag or bow.

Pink in the ear
Sparkling or plain,
Pink on the wrist
Charming or bling,
Pink on the hair
A scarf or a pin,
Pink on the feet
Delicate or boot.

Pink nail colour,
Pink lipstick,
Pink stationery,
Pink ink pens,
Pink pencils or paints,
Pink papers or books,
Pink cards of love,
Pink painted flowers.

Pink in the clouds,
At dawn and dusk,
Pink flecks on the sun,
As it sets or rises,
Pink lakes and sea,
Reflecting the glow,
Pink hue surrounding
The bustling town.

Pink enchants the soul within
As it travels the world so often grey,
Pink anywhere or everywhere too,
Does set it aflutter for a moment or two
Pink does make my soul smile awhile
A pause of delight in its wandering flight.

3. Indigo on white

Indigo on white,
And coal on cream,
In curves, dots and dashes,
Scrolls and twirls,
Seemingly drawing
Innocent lines,
But,
What tales they weave
To think or thrill,
Some so true and
Some not so,
Some of love and
Some of hate,
Tears of laughter or despair,
Calm to soul or fervour to war,
All with a magical wand they weave,
Over readers enthralled,
With all their skill,
What a drab world for the soul to float,
If writers ne'er their swords did wield.

4. Dodging Bullets

Dodging bullets and enemy fire,
Doing the crazy heel-toe dance!
A hop and a skip and twirl away,
Whizzing bullets and shrapnel scatter.
They walk the talk,
The chosen few.
Their anchored soul at peace within,
Through surrounding chaos glides,
Calming, soothing as it passes by,
As Spirit empowered it moves,
Guiding in love courageously,
Own self in peril dangerously.
Many a soul is strengthened,
When these brave ones they do see,
And are inspired to forget their woes
And look to another's need.
In doing so oft they do find,
Themselves all healed and whole,
Left wondering at the miracle,
Of humanity.

5. Dandelion wishes

Scraped knees and dandelion wishes,
Conquered trees and earmarked fruits,
Catapults and caterpillars,
Squirrel nests and birds' eggs,
Tadpoles and guppies
Tyred out from the lake,
Stolen food for stray kittens,
Puppies and some birds,
Jasmine from the fences,
Collected with grace,
Soon skilfully braided,
To jet black hair
By the beach in the summer,
Where frilly waves flowed,
Its frothy white lace,
Burying feet in the sand.
Sandcastles made pretty
With pebbles and shells,
Seawater in buckets,
To fill the moat around!

Nights under the stars with grandma's tales,
Not counting sheep but just falling stars,
Wishing till eyelids tired out closed,
In blissful sleep and many carefree dreams.
Sweet summer days with family and friends,
A tender soul's taste of heaven recollected,
These first steps of the pristine soul,
Remain aglow, softly, never to fade,
A touchstone of grace,
To the wandering soul.

6. Dream catchers

Sacred hymns in choral splendour,
Lullabies of infant slumber,
Sweet melodies of true love strummed,
Joy of laughter in the dance on a drum,
Beats that make idle feet to thump,
To wailing guitars or disco lights' bounce,
Deep sadness of a broken heart is soothed,
Many a time in deep bass and blues,

Grief and loss and many a sigh,
Dream catchers many display in song,
The soul in its truth is moved and lulled,
By Music so varied in this world,
A gift of mercy perhaps from the Gods,
Who kindly look on the human soul,
As its purpose to fulfill it meanders on,
Not knowing it's watched over,
Save through a song.

7. Fireflies

The fireflies on swaying firs,
The fairy lights on garden hedge,
The cat's eyes caught in floodlit glare,
The glow of stars on a moonless night .

The gentle lapping of a lake so still,
The rippling of a flowing stream,
The thundering of a waterfall,
The boom of restless waves on shore.

The rustle of pipal leaves in breeze,
The swish of coconut palms around,
The snap of twigs on swaying trees,
The creak of tree trunks, twisting fro.

The crisp air that chills the face to blush,
The gentle wind that ruffles the hair to brush,
The pristine scents of nature inhaled,
The lightness felt in body and mind.

The soul does thrive when so embraced,
The world of men and lore erased,
The care of nature sends forth refreshed,
The soul to unknown miles, vouchsafed.

8. A symphony of atoms

How precious is the life we have
Within this fragile shell
A symphony of atoms,
Most eloquently designed.

The energy within it,
The aura around it,
The essence of eternity,
Glowing deep inside it.

In the blink of an eye
It is forever lost,
As many a skilled surgeon,
Or sergeant would vouch.

The doctor, the soldier,
And many a priest,
The fleeting glimmer witness,
As quietly it leaves.

The futility of anything
Within human power they know:
Pronounce "Ashes to Ashes,
And dust to dust",
"We did all we could",
"It's not in our hands",
Is often echoed in
Hushed halls of bereavement.

While we the lay people,
So carelessly do,
While away in cares,
And all the ado,
Of stress and tensions,
Targets and commissions;
Let slip through our fingers
This gift of each other.
It's often an unbearable loss that wakes us,
'Never forever' often breaks us,
May God grant wisdom,
And commonsense too,
To value and cherish
From hitherto-
All the lives gifted to us,
To love, care and nourish ,
While the fleeting glow lasts,
Though for a blink.

9. White Light

Loquacious chatterbox
Burble,Piffle, Flumadiddle
Fimble-Famble,Boondoggle, Tiffle
Ferhoodle, Taradiddle.
Aimless chatter, mindless banter,
A lot of nonsense and cavorting,
Is all it seems,
At first glance

Dark curly mop crowning her head,
Doe eyes brimming with mischief ahead
Rosebud lips and dimpled chin,
Noble nose and delicate ears,
Nimble feet, a ballerina's joy,
Hands of sleight, a wizard's ploy.

Hearts go a-flutter or drop dead,
As she wefts through the humdrum life of the world,
Was it a whoosh of angel wings they heard?
Or did they a swish of spiked tail mistake?

Confused, perplexed, they gape awhile,
At the complex being within their walls,
Crowds get dizzy wondering who,
This cherub, minx or vagabond is!

Oblivious to all the whispers she floats,
To graceful tunes her wand she twirls,
With twinkling eyes and smiling lips,
Her master's tapestry she weaves,
Through lives around, a skillful tool,
Self-effacing, precise and charming

Pure light and good is often sensed
As dark and evil in this fallen world,
Yet spotless souls do stumbling find,
A kindred spirit in the one so kind,
And find relief along their way,
With white light so generously displayed.

10. Rainbow

As Keats's dark melancholy,
As Shakespeare's manic tragedy,
As Hamlet's pouted 'skull' brooding,
As Macbeth's wild and mad scheming,
As Coleridge's albatrossed Mariner
As Tennyson's languishing Lotus eaters,
A dark abysmal spiral spinning,
A deep and dark, quick sinking despair.

Resigned to chains of darkness foul,
Restless soul in silence heaving,
Reached feebly to the heavens glowing,
Remembering, whispered prayers all.

And then a wonder of the world did arise,
Afire the 'embered' soul to set,
As Scott's Lochinvar, it swooped swiftly in,
As Kipling's "IF", it gave strength within,

Through rain's prism it viewed white light,
The rainbow displayed in the sky so bright,
The dulled soul's eye did such espy,
The soul gained strength and lifted the die.
The flora washed with gentle showers,
The cheery birdsong in the bowers,
The chains of dark despair broke down,
The soul soared high to light around.

11. Soul kitchen

Golden sunlight on the polished floor,
Making patterns of the latticed door,
Fragrance of coffee fills the air,
Filtered to South Indian perfection,
The smoky hot mix tossed to and fro,
Into waiting cups frothily poured,
Souls awake, nostrils flare,
Eyes closed in peace, the lips do smile,
And taste the morning coffee dear.

The sharp knife glints,
The meshed sieve blinks,
The oft screaming mixer silently waits,
The chimneys gleaming hood,
The icemaker's art cubed,
All await the start of a brand new day.

The cooking vessels, pans and pots,
The cutlery, the crockery and wine glasses tall,
All a beautiful scene portray,
Of sparkling, calm, efficiency,
A belonging, an anchor, secure all day,
It does so oft in one's soul instil,

Tomatoes red, carrots orange,
Lettuce, cucumber, greens aplenty,
Avocados, cherries, an apple or two,
Bananas, musk melons and oranges too,
Sliced chopped or served as whole,
Add colourful cheer to every meal prepared.

The aroma of freshly baked pies or cakes,
The oily fumes of fried fries or meat,
The soft embroidered hand towel and glove,
The scrubber, the wiper and gleeful mop,
Wait expectantly in sweet serenity.

The laughter of family, sharing a meal,
Does joyful respite to one's soul provide,
To live, to love, to laugh, to care,
And rest secure by each other's side;
A dwelling place for sweet repose,
A home where one could safely thrive.

12. Childhood

Sliding down the banister,
Jumping over hedges wide,
Skipping around the garden trees,
Climbing and scraping many a knee,
Stomping in puddles merrily,
Searching for rainbows faithfully.
Sailing paper boats on rainwater flows,
Saving wet kittens and puppies galore,
Waving umbrellas colourful and damp,
Squelching in wet shoes all over the camp.

Giggling inexpressibly,
Laughing irrepressibly,
Prancing around excitedly,
Dancing a tune silently,
Clapping hands wantonly,
Snapping fingers noiselessly,

Pouting sometimes mischievously,
Grinning, winking knowingly,
Singing loud and gloriously,
Reading aloud expressively.
Loving so adoringly,
Caring so perceptively,
Making amends graciously,
Forgiving, hugging limitlessly.

Soul in childhood is heaven filled,
Aging fades it silently,
World worn souls oft mistily,
Recall their true identity,
Wrinkled lines on faces dear,
Filled with love and childish ways,
Restored to pristine selves sincere,
Return to heaven renewed childlike.

13. Walking on air

Walking on air, feet a-flurry,
Willing oneself to a shopping spree,
A bit of retail therapy,
All alone or with the gang,
All agog expectantly,
For a feast of creativity.

The first stop at the gleaming stores,
With their fancy displays and big glass doors,
That slide open so quietly,
To pamper one so blatantly;
The welcoming cool air swirls around,
The high ceilings and space relax the mind;
The wafting perfume fills one with cheer,
To lightly move without a care.
Fabrics, dresses, trousers, coats;
Sequined, printed, embroidered, plain;
Each beckons alluringly,
A whirl of skilful' dressing up'.

Bags and shoes, trinkets and toys,
Perfumes and lipsticks, glossy or matte,
All conspire and enthuse each one;
To believe in beauty thus far unknown;
The queues at billing,
The counters trilling,
The bright bags filling,
The music thrilling,
A mood of conviviality,
A carnival of shopping jollity.

The bustling crowds at the market place,
The colorful wares in open air,
The loud call out of all that's sold,
The bargaining of hagglers a crescendo!
The mood of light effortless fun,
In every human interaction found,
The happy ware admiring crowd,
The beauty of all the things around,
Does lift the cumbered world worn soul,
And makes the heaviest heart feel light,

In shopping sprees and thrifty deals,
In the nooks and corners of our lives,
There's always a hidden nugget to find,
To edify the soul within,
Every day has its gifts to give,
To every soul that would receive,
Received uplifted returns to life,
Feet a-flutter and walking on air.

14. Dream Painters

Dreamers dreaming dripping hues,
Some are partial to the blues,
Dreams so vivid, sharply etched,
Some a blur, in movement brushed.

Earthly flowers, ethereal made,
Wreaths and bouquets from the glade,
Though in their masters' day dream still,
They wait in brush stroked gilt framed sill.

Gardens in all their wondrous splendour,
Lily ponds charms, sweet flora so tender,
White bridges in blue, verde willows slender,
Enchanted, stay dreamlike, in verdant bower.

Portraits of greatness and oft their pets,
Royals and beggars cunningly dealt,
Affluent smooth and hard lined faces,
Distant, endearing, with honest gazes.

Beauties in their cherubic stances,
Statuesque as the pearl drop dances,
Enigmatically the maiden smiles,
As dreamers in paint display their wiles.

Masters and masterpieces all,
Hung in guarded, cold, distant halls,
Do awe and admiration inspire,
Not what the dreamers did aspire.

In the golden glow of a warm hearth,
Amidst the joy of a loving home,
Hangs an unknown dreamer's dream,
Ensconced in trivialities sublime.

Dreamers who with their many hues,
Their dreams and passions in canvas prove,
Though they be masterly pieces now,
Would love the anonymity true,
For many did breathe their last unknown,
To be cherished and loved in a humble home,
Would be their dream, I dream quite so

15. Mortals chasing Immortality

Mortals chasing immortality,
The yearning for eternity,
The longing for 'forever more',
The final 'everlasting life'.

From first breath we tread towards our last,
Steadily through the living world,
Youth disguises mortality,
With its zest, verve and vitality,
Middle age with its dreams achieved,
Lies smugly on its laurel wreaths.

The mortal body shows signs of wear,
Then the mind wakes up to fear,
The mind slowly loses its hold on us,
Then all that's left is our soul within.

Thus we know that's all we are,
Souls travelling through the transient life,
To do the good we're meant to do,
Then close shop and bid adieu.

Those of us who early find,
This truth divine in earthly grind,
Will leave enriched the lives we touch,
Leading to eternity.

As all our forefathers did,
As our pets and all we see did go,
So will we too, seamlessly,
Step into the other world.

Me I rest in grace secure,
That called me to my Savior's side,
My faith assured to life everlasting,
His presence guiding all the way,
When time comes and work here is done,
He'll calm and take me into glory.

16. Dancing Octopus

Age is just a number,
I've heard it said before,
And as my birthday candles grew,
I heard it more and more.
The loving birthday cakes I cut,
Have number candles now,
As I recall, the previous one,
A fire hazard did cause!

Age is just a number
I told myself once more,
And ventured to enhance,
My fading faculties.
Dancing was on the top,
Of my venture list to start;
I did enjoy it in my youth,
And thought it'd be a blast.

I found a class with a kind young thing,
Who impressed me at first call
For she unfazed by my DOB
Did welcome me all heart!
I did my reluctant legs into
Tight leggings old, stuff in,
My shoes and socks,
Did roll their eyes
As my fankles they did meet.

The jolly group I met at class,
Were all young motherlings,
And there I stood my Grandma self
As they welcomed me in!
The instructor did kindly say
"Ma'am you can do slowly"
And I did try to hide myself,
From the mirrors all around me!

My head was working overtime,
As right hand left leg,
Up, down and twirl,
Was all happening all at once.
It had to reset from cassette times,
To MP4 in splits!

The endorphins and the music,
The really good people around,
Did keep me moving with the vibe
And enjoy myself a bit.
And suddenly I caught a glimpse
Of me in the mirror wide!
I looked like a jolly octopus!
Having a whale of a time!

My tentacles I became aware
Could slap a face if I
Careless was and that did
Bring my giggling to a stop.

Age is just a number yes,
I'm grateful mine is large,
As I could not imagine venturing
In my teens to do the same.
Age makes you do some silly things
As you don't mind so much
If a few did get a laugh off you
You'd join them with high fives.
And so I go, old octopus me,
My tentacles to shake,
At least I move like a jellyfish,
And am not a fossil yet!!!

17. Discerning Eye

Grant me the Discerning Eye, O Lord!
To live in this world of two faced men.
The eye to see as clear as crystal,
What's in their heart, not on their lips.

For, if it were so, I'd not be disappointed,
Taken aback or hurt or troubled,
And carry about my life's business,
With the fragile true, though they be few.

And may You grant through Your grace abounding
A heart to love the two-faced ones.
Seal my lips from any guile,
A snide remark, a stab in the back:

Grant me the grace to think well of all,
Knowing some have two faces and all.
Keep me from donning fake faces that flake,
Truthful to thine, may thou me make.

18. Peek-A-Boo

A brush with death, I did not see,
Any good would do to me,
He laughed and said,
"Come on, let's go,
It's just like peek-a-boo."

Though solid on my Rock I stood,
Against the feigning foe,
Oft his cold menacing dance,
Did rattle me to my bones.

But more so, he did play the prank,
On my loved ones all around,
Their worried faces and tear-filled eyes,
I scarce could take no more.

I bade him to my Master come,
And quietly he did,
Squirming he did tell my God,
"Ah! It's just for fun, you see,
I know she's yours and I am just
The clowning courier."
"Hands Off!" I heard, dizzyingly loud,
Roared out in the heavenly hall,
I did feel bad for my foe who fell,
And scrambled away, a wreck.

Now he seems a friendly one,
All reigned in, on a bend,
And lessons many have I learned,
Most hidden from the world.

While chatting with him aimlessly,
When in doldrums we were caught,
He did enlighten me about,
God's grace that kept me free.

In days where all is Life and Love,
And the 'brush' a distant past,
I still know he waits longingly,
To play a game or two.
And sometimes I do wander in,
Into his gaming room,
And play a game of poker or
A bit of 'peek-a-boo'.

19. Masks

Donning masks as social graces,
Dodging, fooling, hustling aces,
Climbing higher in faster paces,
Racing through life's many mazes.

Wearing masks to be a copy,
Greener grass or others' glory,
Never unmasked, the gifted self,
Is often lost in this malaise.

Losing touch with real self thus,
The mask, the person overcomes:
The unknown now the known becomes,
A stranger in the mirror mask-less.

The world awaiting a need to fill,
By masks has lost its fulfilling,
And greater is the tragedy,
A purpose is lost in duplicity.

Preserve each unique identity,
There's just one of each unfathomably,
Mask-less, social graces embrace,
Truth and kindness greatness displays.
Masked, life in false cravings runs,
All gifts and talents lost unused,
Too late hear, Saint Peter say:
"No masks allowed! Game forfeited."

20. Through pink glasses

Sitting on the sidelines
With my dark glasses on,
Watching all the world go by,
Dark, black and dreary.
Grey, grey, grey,
Grey sun, grey sky, grey me!

Head bowed down my gaze did fall
On my limp and dangling feet,
And then I clicked my ruby red shoes,
My glasses turned to pink!
And all the world came bursting forth,
Spinning colours and light around.

The grey men, they turned gallant in puce,
And tall hats nonpareil,
The ladies in gowns of lavender,
And parasols held with flair.

My greyness on the sidelines did,
Transform with my paradigm shift,
My ruby red shoes did dazzle the world,
As nimble on them I twirled.

I scarce could keep my joy within,
It bubbled over in giggling whim,
And spilled over all the world,
As if caught in a merry-go-round,
A topsy-turvy spinning gyre,
As laughter filled the air.

Laughing, happy as a bee,
Buzzing honeyed flights of glee,
Dancing, prancing in a row,
Skipping, sparkling to and fro.
Pulling other sideliners black,
Shift to world of colours back.

Dark or pink,
Our choice it is,
The world turns chameleon!
Pick joy! pick pink! for in a blink,
It will see you through the dark.
Pick black or dark and you will find,
It light would swallow whole,
No glimmer of hope, no ray of light.
Will ever pass through to you.
The way we see the world we live,
Is oft coloured by the lens,
We scarce do grasp the power we have,
We make the world we live..

21. The equalizer

Laughter is the greatest gift,
This world has received yet,
It makes me wonder about my God,
And his thoughts while He did give it.

I realize we've made it a science
And contrived oft do try it
But as we do with most gifts,
We've lost the essence of it.

With AI and the robot clones,
We may master it a bit more,
But in my mind, it will be the last,
To fall to contrived gizmos.

Its essence flows from the soul,
It bubbles forth in sound,
Or sometimes in silence it shows,
In the shaking of a person,
A quintessential human trait,
It's a great equalizer,
Not morose as death which does,
The lesson teach much graver.

A while ago, I did suffer,
With a novel tragedy,
Each time I saw an angry face,
I laughed uncontrollably,
Confused and shocked my opponents did
Often gawk a bit,
Till my tragedy did pass on to them,
And they laughed along with me.
We parted friends most of the time,
Tears streaming from our laughter!!

In hindsight I did realize,
What a saving grace it was!!
Though one or two it did vex more,
Most it diffused to naught.

Laughing at myself sometimes,
Is another cure I find,
Our faux-pas and our foolishness
Become great sources of glee,
And the laughter releases all the stress
When shared with friends and family.

So of all my human faculties
I think I grateful am,
For laughter and that I enjoy,
This gift with all the world.